Text by Lois Rock
Illustrations copyright © 2004 Anna C. Leplar
This edition copyright © 2004 Lion Publishing

The moral rights of the author and illustrator
have been asserted

Published by
Lion Publishing plc
Mayfield House, 256 Banbury Road,
Oxford OX2 7DH, England
www.lion-publishing.co.uk
ISBN 0 7459 4847 2

First edition 2004
1 3 5 7 9 10 8 6 4 2 0

Acknowledgments
The Lord's Prayer from *The Alternative Service Book, 1980* is
copyright © The Central Board of Finance of the Church of England, 1980;
The Archbishops' Council, 1999 and is reproduced by permission.

A catalogue record for this book is available
from the British Library

Typeset in 15/19 Elegant Garamond BT
Printed and bound in Singapore

all about
Prayer

Lois Rock

Illustrated by Anna C. Leplar

LION
Children's Books

What is prayer?

A prayer is something you say to God.

You can say a prayer aloud so other people can hear it.

You can say a prayer in your head so only you and God can hear.

You don't need to use any special words.

Praying to God is like talking to a special friend.

When I talk to you, God,
let me know you are listening.

No one can see God, but Christians believe that God is everywhere.

So you can pray to God anywhere – in quiet places and in crowded places.

It doesn't matter if you're standing up or sitting down, walking along or being still – God can hear your prayer.

Dear God, let me know you are there.

If you want to make a special time to pray, you can go to a place all alone.

There you can really think about what you want to say.

Come close to me, dear God.

When you pray, you can talk to God about anything.
You can talk about the things that make you happy.
You can talk about the things that make you sad.

Dear God, please listen
to all I have to say.

You can tell God about the things you need.
You can tell God about the things you want.

Dear God, bless me
with good things.

You can thank God for all the good things of the world.

Dear God, thank you
for everything.

You can thank God for all the good and clever things you can do.

You can ask God to help you not to get things wrong.

Help me to do good things, dear God, and please forgive me if I forget to.

You can ask God to help other people –
people you know
and people everywhere.

Dear God, bless my family and my friends
and all the people of the world.

If you want to pray but you can't think of what to say, don't worry.

God knows what you want to say. God understands all you are thinking and feeling.

Prayer is trusting that God is with you.

Hear my prayer, dear God,
even when I have no words.

Remember, too, that prayer is listening: listening for
the good thoughts that come from God –
   to help you and guide you
   and to remind you that you are loved.

Dear God, speak to me
in ways I can understand.

Jesus told his friends that God loves to give good things to those who ask in prayer. He said this:

'Ask, and you will receive.

'Seek, and you will find.

'Knock, and the door will be opened to you.'

Answer me, dear God, for I ask
all these things in Jesus' name.

And Jesus gave his friends this prayer:

Our Father, who art in heaven, hallowed be thy name; thy kingdom come; thy will be done; on earth as it is in heaven. Give us this day our daily bread. And forgive us our trespasses, as we forgive those who trespass against us. And lead us not into temptation; but deliver us from evil.

For thine is the kingdom, the power and the glory, for ever and ever. Amen.